Tom and Bella go to feed the hens.

The hens peck the seeds in the grass.

Tom and Bella go into the hut.

Tom and Bella pick up the eggs.

A hen will not get off the nest.

The hen pecks Tom on the chin.

The hen pecks Bella on the cheek.

Oh! Look! The hen has lots of chicks.